DANCERS IN THE GARDEN

by JOANNE RYDER   *Illustrations by* JUDITH LOPEZ

Sierra Club Books for Children
San Francisco

The Sierra Club, founded in 1892 by John Muir, has devoted itself to the study and protection of the earth's scenic and ecological resources — mountains, wetlands, woodlands, wild shores and rivers, deserts and plains. The publishing program of the Sierra Club offers books to the public as a nonprofit educational service in the hope that they may enlarge the public's understanding of the Club's basic concerns. The Sierra Club has some sixty chapters in the United States and in Canada. For information about how you may participate in its programs to preserve wilderness and the quality of life, please address inquiries to Sierra Club, 730 Polk Street, San Francisco, CA 94109.

First Paperback Edition

Acknowledgments
The information in this book is based on observations of Allen's hummingbirds *(Selasphorus sasin)* in several San Francisco gardens — Golden Gate Park's Japanese Tea Garden and Strybing Arboretum, the San Francisco Zoo, and the artist's own garden — and on records of hummingbird behavior, in particular E. C. Aldrich's study of hummingbirds in Berkeley, California, *Natural History of the Allen Hummingbird* (University of California, 1936); *Hummingbirds: Their Life and Behavior,* by Esther Quesada Tyrrell and Robert A. Tyrrell (Crown Publishers, Inc., 1985); and *The Hummingbird Book,* by Donald and Lillian Stokes (Little, Brown and Company, 1989).

Library of Congress Cataloging-in-Publication Data

Ryder, Joanne.
    Dancers in the garden/by Joanne Ryder ; illustrations by Judith Lopez.
        p.   cm.
    Summary: Follows the activities of a hummingbird and his mate in a garden on a sunny day.
    ISBN 0-87156-578-1 (hc)
    ISBN 0-87156-410-6 (pb)
    1. Hummingbirds — Juvenile fiction.   [1. Hummingbirds — Fiction.
2. Birds — Fiction. 3. Gardens — Fiction.]   I. Lopez, Judith, ill.   II. Title.
PZ10.3.R954Dan   1992
[Fic] — dc20   89-10555

Book and cover design by Susan Lu
Printed in Hong Kong
10 9 8 7 6 5 4 3 2 1

For my mother, Dorothy McGaffney Ryder,
who watches and waits for hummingbirds
to visit her garden each year

    JR

For my father

    JL

In the chilly morning,
soft fog paints the garden gray.
Pink petals drift from the trees,
and leaves dangle, damp with dew.

Tucked among the shiny leaves,
a fluffy ball of dark feathers breathes softly.
The tiny bird sleeps so deeply
he does not wake when squirrel races by,
leaping from branch to branch to breakfast.

Quietly the sun rises, spreading its light,
turning the garden green and the pond gold.
Gently the warm sun touches the sleeping bird,
till he stirs, stretching his wings
like a small dark fan, and flies into brightness.
As he dances in the sun,
hummingbird sparkles red, orange, green —
his colors flashing in the morning light.

Dancing in the brightness,
hummingbird dips down
where silken webs dangle,
trapping tiny flyers.
Quickly he plucks a web,
stealing his breakfast from spider.
Then he is gone,
soaring high into the trees.

Young children race through the green garden,
their feet thumping softly across a wooden bridge.
Curious hummingbird dips under the trees,
watching them watch him dance by.
The children laugh, each stretching farther,
trying to touch his bright feathers just out of reach.

Bzzzz . . . bzzzz . . . bzzzz . . .
Through the garden hummingbird dances,
his wings buzzing as he flies.
In the grassy shadows a gray cat listens,
turning her large ears up
to hear the soft whirring beyond *her* reach, too.

In the warm sun, red flowers open like lanterns,
and hummingbird rises to meet them.
He reaches deep inside each flower
with his thin, dark bill
and quickly licks the sweet nectar
with his long, long tongue.

Hummingbird dances from flower to flower,
hanging in space, pausing in mid-air,
his wings blurring, beating too fast to see.
No one dances quite like hummingbird —
forward, backward, even upside down!

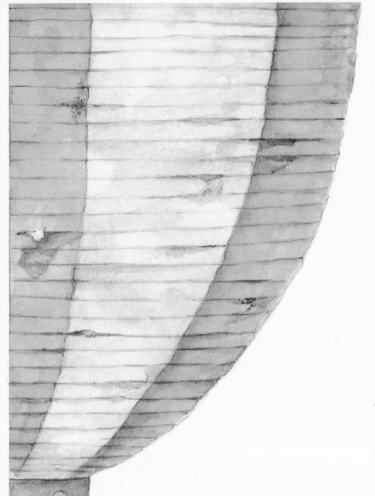

Bzzzz . . . bzzzzz.
Another bright bird dances near the red flowers.
He does not see hummingbird watching him.
Zeet . . . zeet, hummingbird calls angrily.
He darts back and forth,
his tail spread wide, buzzing and chasing,
till the stranger flies over a fence.
Then he rests, calling, *Tick . . . tick . . . tick,*
telling all birds, *This is my garden.*
These are my flowers.

In the warmth of the day, hummingbird dances
near a fountain, bathing in its cool spray.
The clean wet bird perches in a patch of sun,
smoothing his bright feathers with his long bill.

At the edge of the garden,
trees stand tall.
Within their graceful branches,
a small bird tucks her nest.
She weaves together
soft feathers and strong grass,
green moss and pale spiderwebs
to make a tiny cup.
And when she's done,
she dances down,
  down to the garden . . .

Tick . . . tick . . . tick,
hummingbird calls, ready to chase her away.
But then he stops . . . and flies above her.
He does a special dance, dipping and rising,
his feathers buzzing, his feathers sparkling.
Zeeka . . . zeeka . . . zeeka, she calls to him.
And he flies higher, then dives —
falling quickly, buzzing loudly — from the sky.
He dips and soars again and again,
dancing a fast wild dance — just for her.

At last he buzzes closer,
darting back and forth in front of her,
till both fly off, dancing in the sunlight,
to a shadowy place where they mate.

Then the hummingbirds part —
one to his flowers, one to her nest.
She rests by the small mossy cup
till hawk circles, gliding too near,
and she chases him far,
far away from the home
she has made for her young.

As the sun creeps behind the tall trees,
animals find places to rest in the shadowy garden.
Hummingbird buzzes from flower to flower,
eating his last meal of this spring day.

Then he rests too,
closing his eyes, folding his wings,
till he's small and dark like the small dark leaves
that dance around him in the cool evening breeze.

And in the tall trees, a small bird sleeps in her nest.
Soon she will lay a tiny white egg, then another.
Before long, there will be more hummingbirds
whirring and dancing in the bright sun.

Dancers in *your* garden

When I was a child, no hummingbirds lived in our New York garden. But each year we saw one or two of these smallest of birds migrating south. My mother started looking for them each August. I can still remember her calling, "Oh, come quickly. There's a hummingbird outside."

Now I live in California and I see hummingbirds often, but each one still seems like a small gift to treasure and remember.

When you first glimpse a hummingbird, you might think it is an insect — perhaps a big hovering bee — rather than a bird. You may hear the humming of its wings before you see it. It beats its wings so quickly, they blur as you watch. Some hummingbirds beat their wings nearly 80 times a second!

As a male hummingbird flies toward you, the feathers on his throat may dazzle like jewels. These feathers are iridescent. They have no pigment in them, but they reflect colors from the sunlight. You will see the brilliant colors best if the sun is behind you and the hummingbird is facing the sun. When the bird turns or flies into the shadows, you may see the colors change or even disappear, until the bird's bright throat looks black.

Some male hummingbirds perform elaborate aerial diving displays. A male displays to let others — males, females, and even humans — know this is his territory. He may also display to encourage a female to stay and mate. She may be visiting his territory looking for food, nesting materials, or a mate.

After mating, the female returns to her nest and lays two white eggs, a day or two apart. The eggs — half the size of jellybeans — hatch in two to three weeks. The mother hummingbird will take care of her young alone.

A hummingbird's tiny body works at an incredibly fast rate. Its heart can beat more than 1200 times per minute — many times faster than a human heart.

To produce the energy it needs to live and fly, a hummingbird eats many short meals during the day. It feeds about every ten to twelve minutes, for a minute or less at a time. Its diet consists of nectar and small insects and spiders. Some hummingbirds feed more frequently at day's end, storing up energy for the long night.

On chilly nights or when food is scarce, a hummingbird can survive by going into a resting state called torpor. In this state, its heartbeat and breathing slow down and its body temperature is lowered. It uses up much less energy than normal. In the morning, it may awake slowly, warming as the temperature around it rises.

If there are hummingbirds in your area, it's fun to become a hummingbird-watcher. Try to find a blooming plant where they like to feed — they are often attracted to long red flowers. Hummingbirds can reach deep inside flowers with their thin bills and lick the hidden nectar with their long tongues. As they feed, hummingbirds carry pollen from one flower to another, helping to pollinate plants.

You may be able to attract local or migrating hummingbirds by planting certain flowers or by putting a red hummingbird feeder in your garden. Mix one part white sugar to four parts water, stir until the sugar is well dissolved, and fill your feeder. Every two or three days, clean the feeder and refill it with fresh sugar water. It is important to change the mixture frequently. Left too long, sugar water will spoil and may endanger the health of feeding birds. Also, do not use honey in your mixture. Honey does not dissolve well in water and can be extremely harmful to hummingbirds.

A hummingbird may come to a feeder or bush, feed for a few moments, and then fly away to rest nearby. It may return to the same place to eat several times in an hour. Most of its day is spent resting between periods of activity.

Watching hummingbirds requires patience, for each observation may be brief. But there is something very special about catching a glimpse of these amazing and beautiful flyers.

Happy hummingbird-watching!